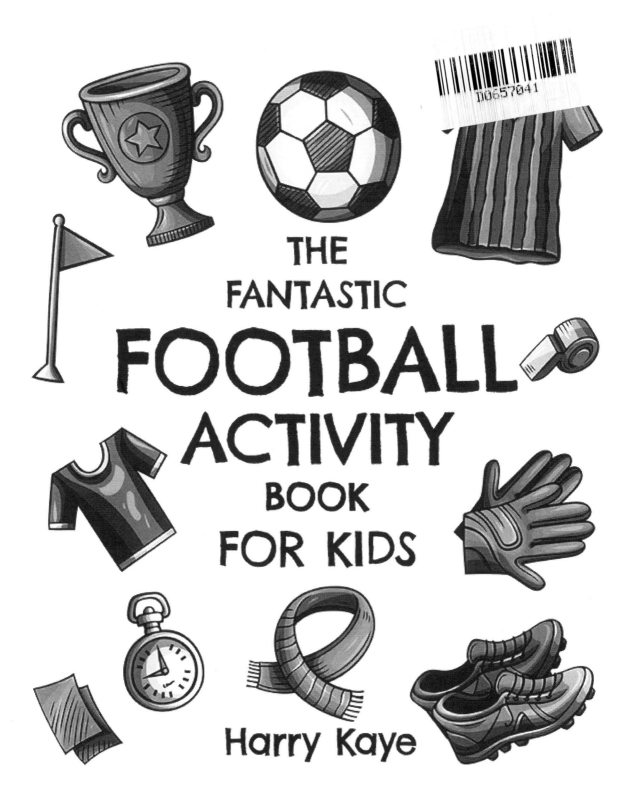

THE
FANTASTIC
FOOTBALL
ACTIVITY
BOOK
FOR KIDS

Harry Kaye

Publisher Information

Published by Harry Kaye Books

Copyright © 2019 Harry Kaye

This book is an unofficial publication and is not authorised in any way by any of the football clubs mentioned. The information should be accurate as of the time of publishing. If you disagree, let us know!

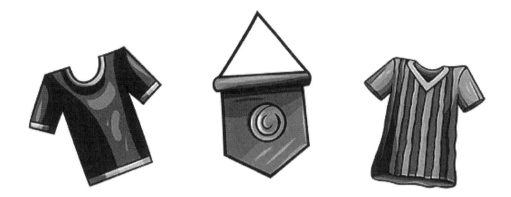

THIS BOOK
BELONGS TO

_____

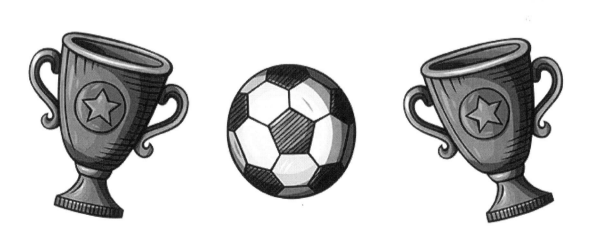

What's in the Book?

Colour in the Player #1

Colour in the image below. The player is about to score a great goal!

Your Ultimate Team

Who would play in your ultimate team? Messi, Ronaldo, Kane, Bronze? Don't forget to add yourself in your favourite position.

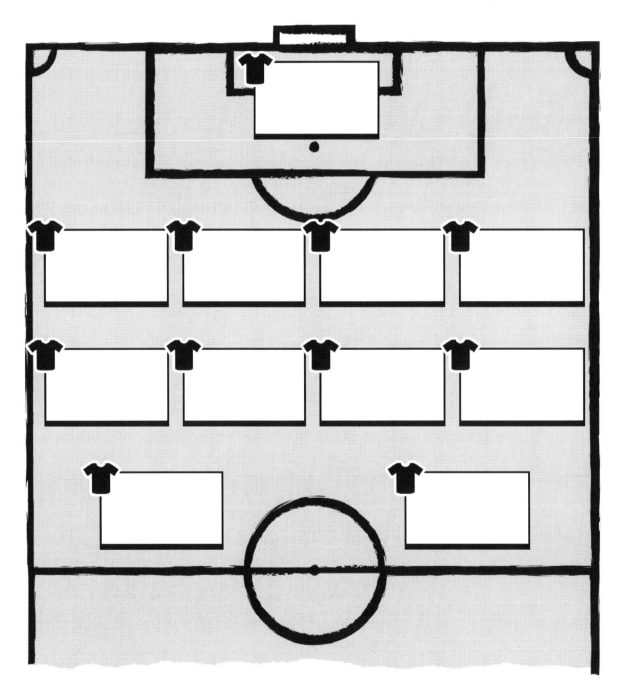

Football Maths #1

⚽ = 2 🏆 = 3 👕 = 1

👕 + ⚽ = _____

⚽ + ⚽ + 3 = _____

⚽ + 🏆 + 1 = _____

⚽ + 🏆 + 👕 = _____

🏆 + 🏆 - 1 = _____

2 + 👕 + 🏆 + 1 = _____

Answers on page 63

Where on the Map?
Football Stadiums

On the opposite page is a map of England, Scotland and Wales. Each of the numbers is a famous football team's stadium. Can you match the teams below with their stadiums?

Liverpool's stadium is number   _____

Norwich City's stadium is number   _____

Arsenal's stadium is number   _____

Cardiff City's stadium is number   _____

Aston Villa's stadium is number   _____

Southampton's stadium is number   _____

Leicester City's stadium is number   _____

Celtic's stadium is number   _____

Newcastle United's stadium is number   _____

Answers on page 67

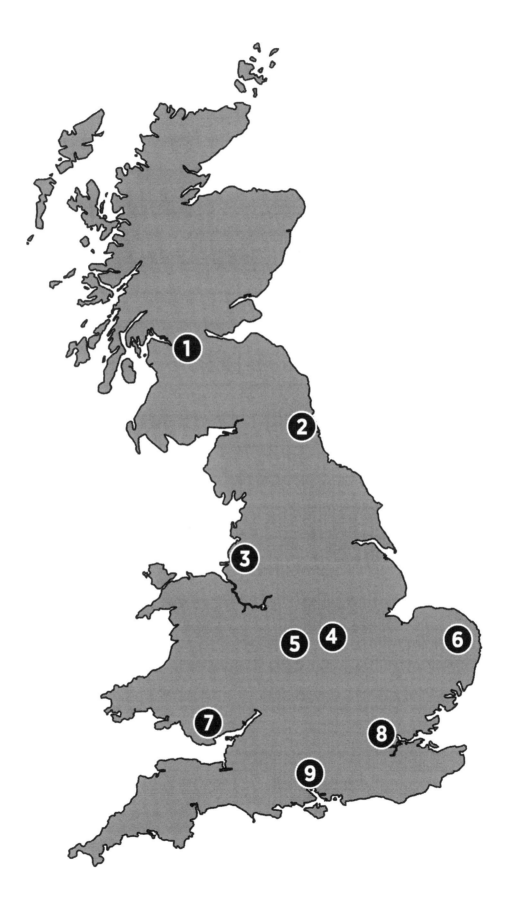

Top Players Word Search #1

Can you find some of the world's best players in the word search?

```
B D R U M Z K C E A X C B O C F D
P L N H H A V G L D I V B R R O D
D W N X X R R A P R S R Z G I U R
V Z R X O X L C D B E J N O S T A
K L L Q J I R O E C N O N D T G Z
E Y B I S H M A P L J E X G I I A
S T L S O A P X T E O K T S A L H
E B O I K N R H D Z S L I G N E N
R N W U A Y E E P O B C C E O D E
G H L D L N I L H T Q F A K R S D
I V X D G K M R M W I I D H O J E
O A P P N G L B O E W A Q Z N I C
R U G E G F O Z A W S U Z G A H Q
A X R J W O F E W P J S L X L T Y
M F B E J Q A K G A P M I B D T H
O S G V R C P R J F O E S C O A C
S Y V I R G I L V A N D I J K M G
```

Alisson, Matthijs de Ligt, Marcelo, Sergio Ramos, Virgil van Dijk, Frenkie de Jong, Eden Hazard, Luka Modric, Cristiano Ronaldo, Kylian Mbappe, Lionel Messi

Answers on page 84

Secret Code Teams

On this page are the names of five football clubs. They've been translated into a secret code! Use the table below, which lists all the letters from A to Z and their "secret code", to work out the club names. Good luck!

A	B	C	D	E	F	G	H	I	J	K	L	M	N	O	P	Q	R	S	T	U	V	W	X	Y	Z
M	T	C	E	F	S	O	L	I	D	P	B	A	W	U	V	N	R	Y	Z	G	X	H	Q	K	J

E O H W M A

_ _ _ _ _ _

M R F D Q M H

_ _ _ _ _ _ _

Q D N C M F B H D   O Q I B D J

_ _ _ _ _ _ _ _ _   _ _ _ _ _ _

N D F B   W M A   O Q I B D J

_ _ _ _   _ _ _   _ _ _ _ _ _

Q G B B I Q U W M A   E G R D F B

_ _ _ _ _ _ _ _ _ _   _ _ _ _ _ _

Answers on page 77

Match the Silhouettes

Can you draw a line between the players on this page and their silhouette on the next page?

Answer on page 69

Mixed Up Keepers

The names of these goalkeepers have been mixed up.

Can you unravel them?

1. A Peak Grail Bazaar _____

2. Unsung Nag _____

3. A Diva Edged _____

4. Sore Ned _____

5. Hurl Igloos _____

6. A Cop Drink Fjord _____

7. Hip Mackerel Chess _____

8. In Lasso _____

Answers on page 75

Chase for the Ball!

Bobby needs to reach the ball in the centre before his friends.
Can you find the right path through the maze?

Answer on page 84

The Internationals

These are some of the best players in the world. But which teams did they play international football for?

1	Antoine Griezmann	Algeria
2	Luis Suárez	Belgium
3	Eden Hazard	Colombia
4	James Rodríguez	Egypt
5	David De Gea	France
6	Mo Salah	Gabon
7	Riyad Mahrez	Spain
8	Zlatan Ibrahimovic	Sweden
9	Pierre-Emerick Aubameyang	Uruguay

Answers on page 79

England's Missing Letters

We've stolen some consonants from the names of famous England players. Can you work out who they are?

1. _A___ MA_UI_E

2. DE_E A__I

3. _A_EEM _TE__I__

4. _O__ _TO_E_

5. _A___ _A_E

6. _O__ _A___E_

7. MA__U_ _A___O_D

8. _ADO_ _A___O

Answers on page 78

Design a Football Kit

Your favourite team needs a new kit. Can you design a really cool one for them?

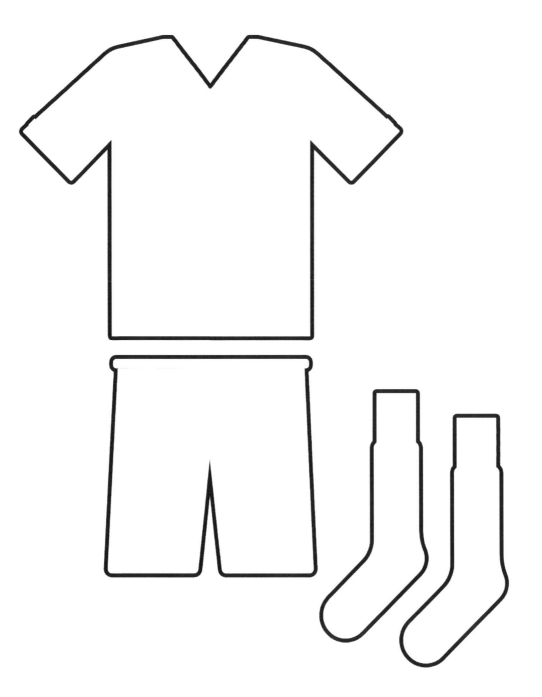

Beat the Clock – AAA!

You have ten minutes! Can you write down twenty football teams with the letter A in their names? Ten is impressive, twenty would be amazing!

1 _____

2 _____

3 _____

4 _____

5 _____

6 _____

7 _____

8 _____

9 _____

10 _____

11 _____

12 _____

13 _____

14 _____

15 _____

16 _____

17 _____

18 _____

19 _____

20 _____

Football Talk #1

"Germany are a very difficult team to play... they had eleven internationals out there today."

- STEVE LOMAS
(Man City, West Ham)

Internationals? In an international team? Whatever next?!

"I always used to put my right boot on first, and then obviously my right sock."

- BARRY VENISON
(Sunderland, Liverpool, Newcastle)

So, boot... then... sock? Don't try that at home, kids!

"I'd like to play for an Italian club, like Barcelona."

- MARK DRAPER
(Notts County, Aston Villa)

So, that's Barcelona in... SPAIN!

"The first ninety minutes of a football match are the most important."

- BOBBY ROBSON
(ex-England Manager)

Surely the last ninety are just as important?

Your Favourite Team

○ Name

_____

○ Stadium

_____

○ Manager

_____

○ Best Current Player

_____

○ Best Player of all time

_____

○ Who should they sign?

_____

○ First game you watched

_____

○ Best Game

_____

Matchday Bingo

Next time you watch a big match, tick off the events below!

The Referee checks their watch

Substitution

A fantastic save!

Offside

A shot hits the bar or post

A yellow or red card

A corner is taken

GOAL! Your team scores!!

The ref blows their whistle

Match the Pairs

Each shirt has an exact match somewhere on this page – Can you draw a line between each matching pair of shirts?

Answers on page 82

Spot the Cliché

Footballers, managers and pundits often say the same silly phrases over and over again. These are called clichés, but can you spot which ones are real, and which we've made up?

Sick as a parrot?   Or   Sick as a goat?

He plays box to box   Or   He plays corner to corner?

A game of half and half   Or   A game of two halves?

Early doors   Or   Late doors?

Parking the car   Or   Parking the bus?

Hit the crossword   Or   Hit the woodwork?

Kick it in Row Z   Or   Kick it in Row A?

Running down the wall   Or   Running down the clock?

A windy Wednesday in Wales   Or   A wet Tuesday night in Stoke?

Answers on page 71

Top Teams Word Search #1

Can you find the football teams at the bottom of the page?

```
D E T I N U R E T S E H C N A M T
N V H Y N H C V U P K I O R N S P
O Q G T L P V E Z F E S O A M H D
R A U N S V P L R C T T X N I E Y
W I O U V A X Z I M Q U C L Z F T
I B R O N R R D U F D H J E Z F I
C F B C T O L S W W E Q T R Y I C
H C S Y M W T B E V I R Q K D E R
C P E B M U T P G N A X O J B L E
I N L R O V Y L M R A C B L U D T
T A D E N H W P C A E L G T P U S
Y K D D J C E C J F H A X O B N E
K D I X J O P M P A G T P O N I C
M D M Q R K J G U T I Z U V R T I
E V O T X Z W V I L K V A O K E E
D E T I N U M A H T S E W B S D L
D E T I N U S D E E L Q Y P C C F
```

Manchester United, Arsenal, West Ham United, Leeds United, Middlesbrough, Derby County, Sheffield United, Southampton, Leicester City, Norwich City

Answers on page 90

Name That Team #1

Team 1

Their main kit is dark blue.

They play at Goodison Park.

Their nickname is the Toffees.

Seamus Coleman and Wayne Rooney have played for them.

Team 1 is _____

Team 2

Their main kit is Yellow.

They play at Carrow Road.

Their nickname is the Canaries.

Teemu Pukki and Tim Krul have played for them.

Team 2 is _____

Answers on page 69

Colouring Time!

Can you colour in the picture of the footballer below?

Premier League Word Search

Find the players who've played in the Premier League.

```
O S E L P V S E V E N N E B U R S
M R K W I L F R E D N D I D I N D
M M A C K S J G H B O W D X L Z I
L H N K Y F N M X Z B T R E A O K
E S A X Q U H I E N Q F C C I N J
A N H S L U C K A P X Y P I T Z R
G N T B K G Y B A G K F U R R A K
W N A K A H X T I N A R G N A L U
X B N M J W O T W E Q U T A M U P
L Z D N K K M L L S V Q M L Y C W
B J K V H L H Q H W J E A C N A A
Y Z E M O G E O J U Q K T E O S U
X E E J Q P C L F P I G Z D H M T
C B E R N A R D O S I L V A T O G
F J W N G G R G H Q B X A V N U R
Y Z W I P L K B R A K Y Z D A R A
G I K D V M A H A R B A Y M M A T
```

Nathan Aké, Bernardo Silva, Rúben Neves, Anthony Martial, Lucas Moura, Tammy Abraham, Granit Xhaka, Joe Gomez, Wilfred Ndidi, Declan Rice

Answers on page 89

Football Maths #2

 + ⚑ = ____

2 + ⚑ + 🐚 = ____

🏆 - 3 + ⚑ - 2 = ____

🏆 + 🏆 - ⚑ = ____

🏆 + 🏆 - 1 = ____

(2 x ⚑) + 🏆 = ____

Answers on page 64

Spot the Difference

There are eleven differences between the picture on this page and the next. Can you find all of them?

Differences:

1. _____

2. _____

3. _____

4. _____

5. _____

6. _____

7. _____

8. _____

9. _____

10. _____

11. _____

Answers on page 70

Design a Club Crest

You've decided to launch your own football club, and need a new crest for your team's shirts. Colour in the best crest you can on this page.

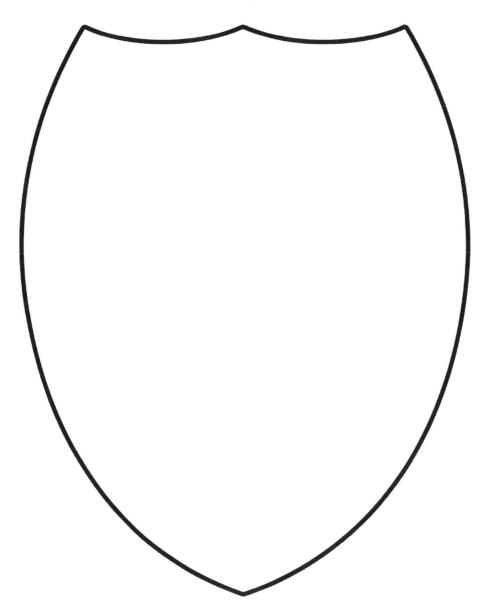

Find Words From a Word #1

FOOTBALLERS

Using just the letters in the word FOOTBALLERS, how many words can you make? Give yourself 2 points for any two letter words, 3 points for three letters words, 4 points for ... ok, you should have worked out how many by now. Good luck!

_____

_____

_____

_____

_____

_____

How Many Balls?

There are four different ball designs in the image. Can you count how many of each design there are, and write the answers in the boxes?

Answers on page 70

The Perfect Player

Can you combine all your favourite players into one perfect footballer? Write down who you think is best in each box.

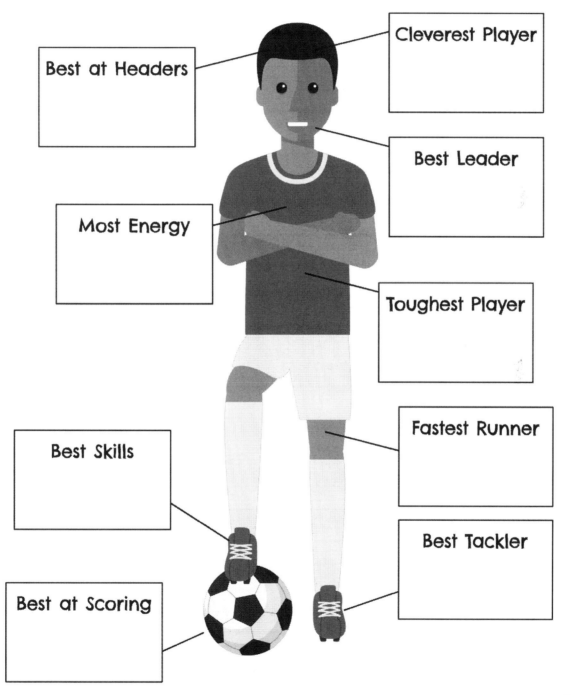

Best at Headers

Cleverest Player

Best Leader

Most Energy

Toughest Player

Best Skills

Fastest Runner

Best Tackler

Best at Scoring

Secret Code Honours

On this page are the names of five Championships or Cups. They've been translated into a secret code! Use the table below, which lists all the letters from A to Z and their "secret code", to work out the names. Good luck!

A	B	C	D	E	F	G	H	I	J	K	L	M	N	O	P	Q	R	S	T	U	V	W	X	Y	Z
D	E	Y	W	F	H	A	Z	K	V	S	M	N	I	L	G	X	J	O	T	U	Q	P	R	B	C

EG   ZUW

_ _   _ _ _

BUXSWG   OBGPUB

_ _ _ _ _ _   _ _ _ _ _ _

WXBLNBX   OBGPUB

_ _ _ _ _ _ _   _ _ _ _ _ _

DSXOA   ZUW

_ _ _ _ _   _ _ _

ZFGLWNSMK   OBGPUB

_ _ _ _ _ _ _ _ _   _ _ _ _ _ _

Answer on page 80

Design a Cup

The FA want you to design a new cup for them. Colour in the one below to show them your skills!

Where on the Map?
European Teams

On the opposite page is a map of Europe. Each number is an international football team, but which number matches which team?

Spain is country number   _____

Wales is country number   _____

Sweden is country number   _____

Portugal is country number   _____

Scotland is country number   _____

Italy is country number   _____

Northern Ireland is country number   _____

France is country number   _____

England is country number   _____

Germany is country number   _____

Republic of Ireland is country number   _____

Answers on page 68

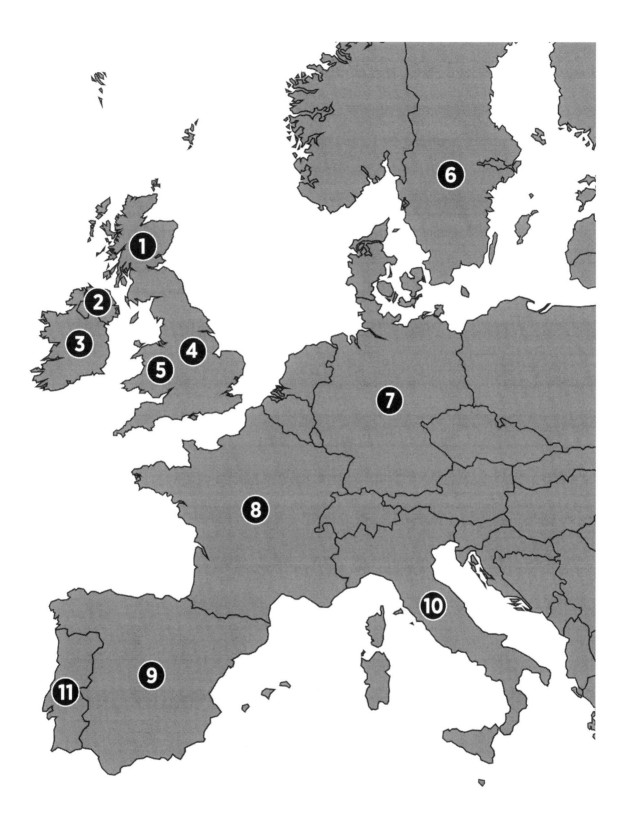

Football Talk #2

"The thing about goalscorers is that they score goals"

- TONY COTTEE
(West Ham, Everton)

You know what? – he's right too!

"I don't think there is anybody bigger or smaller than Maradona."

- KEVIN KEEGAN
(ex-England Manager)

Really? Doesn't that mean everyone is the same size as Maradona? That seems very unlikely!

"Both sides have scored a couple of goals, and both sides have conceded a couple of goals."

- PETER WITH
(Aston Villa)

Well, that adds up.

"For those of you watching in black and white, Spurs are in the all-yellow strip."

JOHN MOTSON
(TV Commentator)

In the olden days TV was black and white, just like this book – and yellow was definitely not black and white.

Name That Team #2

Team 3

Their main kit is white shirt and blue shorts.

Their ground is called Gigg Lane.

Their nickname is the Shakers.

They were expelled from the Football League in 2019.

Team 3 is _____

Team 4

Their main kit is red and white stripes.

They play at St Mary's Stadium.

Their nickname is the Saints.

Ryan Bertrand and Gareth Bale have played for them.

Team 4 is _____

Answers on page 75

Which Line? Can You Score?

Which line should Ellie follow if she wants to score a goal?

I think Ellie should choose line ___

The answer is on page 69

European Teams Word Search

Can you find some of the Europe's best teams in the word search?

```
Y  U  A  Z  I  U  H  M  S  Z  S  D  F  U  M  M  R
J  C  T  N  R  Y  E  H  J  U  C  H  E  I  O  F  P
Z  D  L  K  Z  M  E  G  T  Z  W  G  C  B  A  P  N
B  S  E  Y  P  F  Q  N  O  J  X  X  M  F  C  U  T
A  H  T  K  S  L  E  U  R  X  Y  Y  W  D  U  E  H
R  Z  I  W  E  V  P  K  W  O  A  B  I  E  O  L  C
C  B  C  M  U  Y  H  P  I  S  A  R  X  C  T  J  I
E  W  O  J  L  H  V  L  J  O  D  E  Q  O  D  M  N
L  S  M  T  W  P  O  H  W  A  T  R  L  L  D  N  U
O  Y  A  B  U  P  N  T  M  V  L  R  W  P  U  T  M
N  A  D  B  A  O  K  L  F  E  Y  J  O  Q  R  C  N
A  N  R  H  J  A  J  Y  V  V  B  I  P  T  D  R
D  H  I  W  Z  E  S  S  O  N  M  P  O  A  A  U  E
F  Y  D  E  R  W  Q  H  J  S  E  V  I  L  L  A  Y
D  N  U  M  T  R  O  D  A  I  S  S  U  R  O  B  A
X  Q  T  W  M  O  Y  U  I  B  Y  P  Y  X  I  R  B
P  A  R  I  S  S  A  I  N  T  G  E  R  M  A  I  N
```

Barcelona, Bayern Munich, Juventus, Atlético Madrid, Paris Saint-Germain, Real Madrid, Borussia Dortmund, Napoli, Porto, Sevilla

Answers on page 92

Football Maths #3

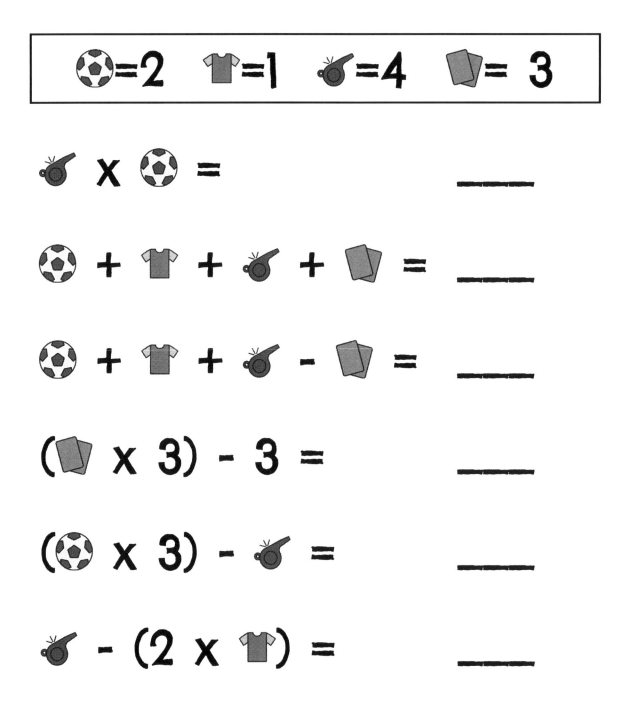

⚽=2   👕=1   📯=4   🟦= 3

📯 x ⚽ =   ____

⚽ + 👕 + 📯 + 🟦 = ____

⚽ + 👕 + 📯 - 🟦 = ____

(🟦 x 3) - 3 =   ____

(⚽ x 3) - 📯 =   ____

📯 - (2 x 👕) =   ____

Answers on page 65

Colouring Skills!

Can you colour in the picture below?

Find the Player

Can you find Aiden Maguire, the top football player? Follow the clues to work out which of the people on the opposite page is Aiden. Put a cross next to any player you know isn't Aiden and, by the end of the clues, you should just have one footballer left!

Clue #1   Aiden isn't wearing glasses

Clue #2   Aiden isn't holding a trophy.

Clue #3   Aiden doesn't have a beard.

Clue #4   Aiden has a ball

Clue #5   Aiden isn't waving

Clue #6   Aiden hasn't got his arms crossed.

Clue #7   Aiden isn't holding a ball in his hands.

Clue #8   Aiden doesn't have his foot on his ball.

If you've found Aiden, congratulations – if not, go back to the start and make sure you follow the clues exactly!

Answer on page 73

The Tricky Maze Cup

Can you find your way to the centre of this tricky maze?
If you can, you'll win the cup?

Answer on page 72

Design a Pair of Boots

All footballers love a cool pair of boots. Can you colour in the ones below so that they look fantastic?

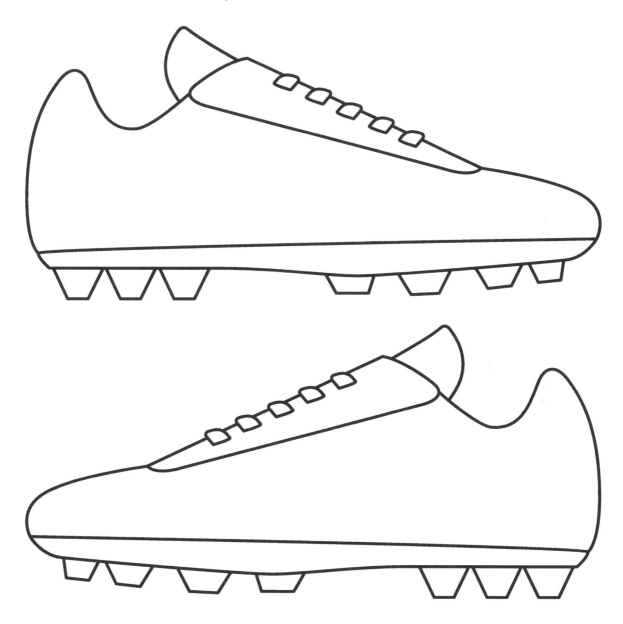

Find Words From a Word #2

GOALKEEPERS

Using just the letters in the word GOALKEEPERS, how many words can you make? Give yourself 2 points for any two letter words, 3 points for three letters words, 4 points for ... ok, you should have worked out how many by now. Good luck!

Beat the Clock – England!

You have ten minutes! Can you write down twenty players who have played for England?

Ten would be good, fifteen amazing and twenty means you're a superfan!

1 _____

2 _____

3 _____

4 _____

5 _____

6 _____

7 _____

8 _____

9 _____

10 _____

11 _____

12 _____

13 _____

14 _____

15 _____

16 _____

17 _____

18 _____

19 _____

20 _____

Beat the Defenders!

Find your way through the maze and score a goal – but you need to avoid the defenders on your way!

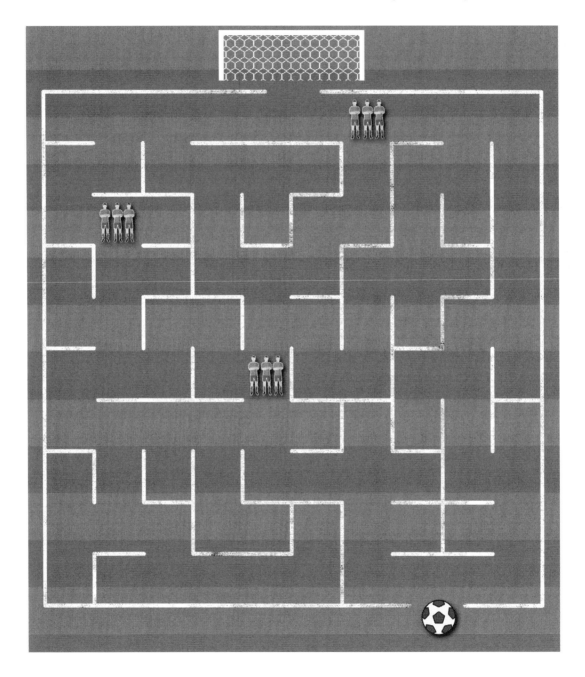

Answer on page 74

Top Players Word Search #2

Can you find some of the world's best players in the word search?

```
A D R A N E R E I D N E W Z V T F
S D L M W V N F O W C Q D W A W A
E E J A L U C Y B R O N Z E F U U
L Z Z N X M E G A N R A P I N O E
L Z N D X Z J Q E C U Q Z Y P D E
E E A I G U E D V A D Z T J J U E
V I T N B I G Z H Q A P R L S J C
A R Z E F V D F C L Y K E F U K J
L T U H S N Y B E H A J E N Z R E
E P D E M W Z X F O Y K I J C Q L
S B A N R A M V L A P F L T D E V
O K E R F O R Y E W D T U Z Z S E
R O R Y R O X T T F J V J G B R R
C G X G N I L L A F I S C H E R V
K B A R V G W T K S W D S W V W K
M N L I G K E L L E Y O H A R A Q
S A R I V A N V E E N E N D A A L
```

Sari van Veenendaal, Lucy Bronze, Nilla Fischer, Kelley O'Hara,
Wendie Renard, Julie Ertz, Amandine Henry, Rose Lavelle, Marta,
Alex Morgan, Megan Rapinoe

Answers on page 87

Mixed Up Teams

The names of these football teams have been mixed up.

Can you unravel them?

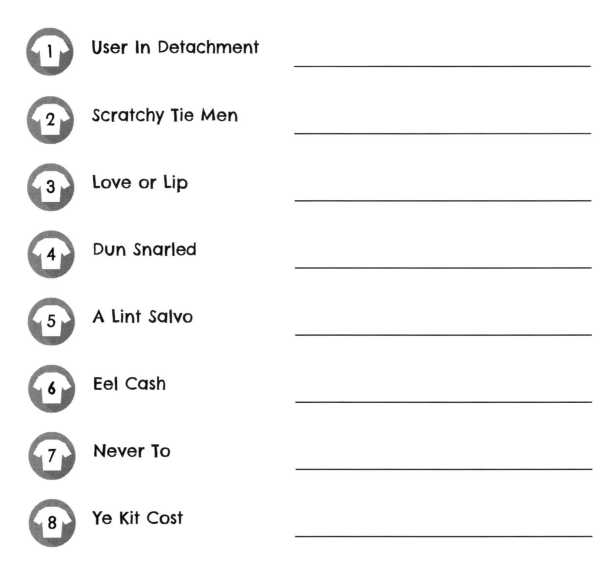

1. User In Detachment _____

2. Scratchy Tie Men _____

3. Love or Lip _____

4. Dun Snarled _____

5. A Lint Salvo _____

6. Eel Cash _____

7. Never To _____

8. Ye Kit Cost _____

Answers on page 81

Football Talk #3

"If you closed your eyes, you couldn't tell the difference between the two sides"

PHIL BROWN
(ex-Hull and Southend Manager)

True. If I close my eyes I can't really tell what's going on at all in football matches.

"He dribbles a lot and the opposition don't like it - you can see it all over their faces."

- RON ATKINSON
(ex-Man United and Aston Villa Manager)

Er... Yuck!

"I couldn't settle in Italy. It was like living in a foreign country."

- IAN RUSH
(Liverpool and, briefly, Juventus)

So, Italy, the foreign country, was like a foreign country?

"They're the second best team in the world, and there's no higher praise than that."

- KEVIN KEEGAN
(ex-England Manager)

Nothing better than second best? Maybe "first" best?

Teams with Missing Letters

We've stolen all the consonants from the names of some famous football teams. Can you work out who they are?

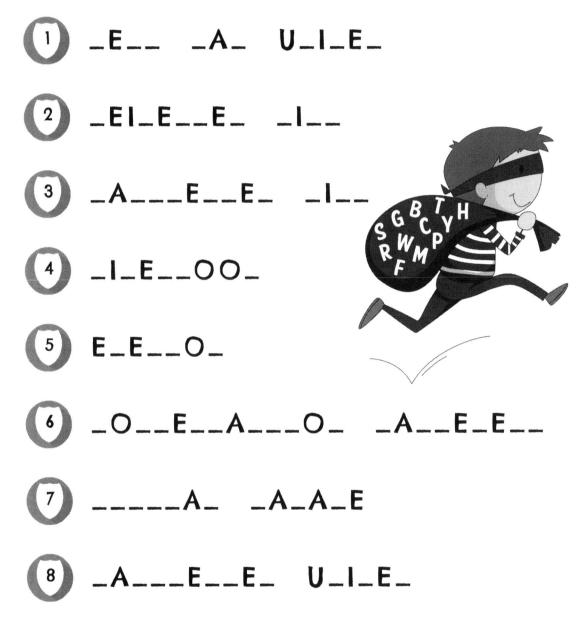

1. _E_ _ _A_ U_I_E_

2. _EI_E_ _E_ _I_ _

3. _A_ _ _E_ _E_ _I_ _

4. _I_E_ _OO_

5. E_E_ _O_

6. _O_ _E_ _A_ _ _O_ _A_ _E_E_ _

7. _ _ _ _ _A_ _A_A_E

8. _A_ _ _E_ _E_ U_I_E_

Answers on page 83

Which Stadium?

On the left is a list of football teams. On the right is a list of stadiums – can you match the team to the correct stadium?

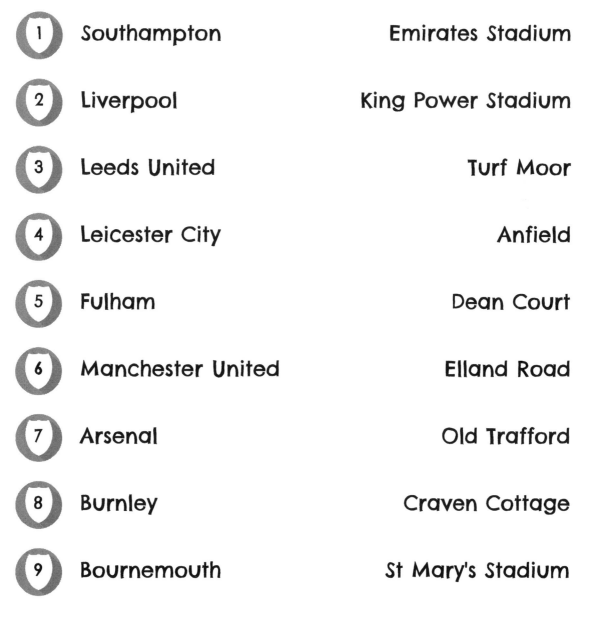

1	Southampton	Emirates Stadium
2	Liverpool	King Power Stadium
3	Leeds United	Turf Moor
4	Leicester City	Anfield
5	Fulham	Dean Court
6	Manchester United	Elland Road
7	Arsenal	Old Trafford
8	Burnley	Craven Cottage
9	Bournemouth	St Mary's Stadium

Answers on page 76

Name That Team #3

Team 5

Their main kit is light blue.

They play at the Etihad.

Their nickname is the Citizens.

David Silva and Yaya Toure have played for them.

Team 5 is _____

Team 6

Their main kit is white.

They play at Elland Road.

They were English Champions in 1992.

Liam Cooper and Lee Bowyer have played for them.

Team 6 is _____

Answers on page 83

Secret Code Players

On this page are the names of five footballers. They've been translated into a secret code! Use the table below, which lists all the letters from A to Z and their "secret code", to work out the players' names. Good luck!

U	V	T	P	S	H	Y	N	Q	B	W	X	R	F	D	M	J	O	I	K	G	E	Z	A	C	L

⇑ ⌣ ⊢ ↻ ⇧ ↻ ⋏ ⊢   ↻ ⌣ ⊢ ↺ ⊬

_ _ _ _ _ _ _ _   _ _ _ _

⇧ ⇧ ⇐ ⇐ ↳ ↻   ⇈ ⋏ ⇐ ⇈ ↺ ⊢

_ _ _ _ _ _   _ _ _ _ _

⇧ ⇐ ⌣ ∩   ⋏ ⇈ ↺ ⇑ ⋏

_ _ _ _   _ _ _ _ _

⇑ ⌣ ⊢   ⇧ ↳ ⋏ ⇐ ⇈ ⌣ ⇐ ⇐

_ _ _   _ _ _ _ _ _ _ _

↻ ↺ ⇈ ⇈   ⇑ ⇧ ↻ ∧ ⇐ ⌣ ⊬

_ _ _ _   _ _ _ _ _ _ _

Answer on page 86

Stadiums Word Search

Can you find the stadiums at the bottom of the page?

```
S T A M F O R D B R I D G E T S K
A P T H E H A W T H O R N S K I I
C V V M T N J Y P T W J G R V L R
W P K Z Q V M X B B C K A V U C K
L C F G Y R A L B Y R P B V V K L
K B R V X H G W X A N D C J V R E
E L X Z F A K H P O A G R F X A E
S R Z Q T U L S S O D E V D A P S
T K H P H J E I R A Z D N K K T S
B M P C X M D E O X I P R C G S T
H U F Y A O G R O Z K A S U N R A
T O X J O A W A E F P J D I X U D
O J T G R O K D L A H A U X D H I
A S F A R Y F D L N E N F Z A L U
Z N C R Y Z R L E J V M H J W E M
R I A M O L I N E U X N I Z O S C
V C W S C V B Q H E E M S K M S J
```

St James' Park, Vicarage Road, Villa Park, Stamford Bridge, Kirklees Stadium, Goodison Park, Molineux, Carrow Road, Selhurst Park, The Hawthorns

Answers on page 91

Football Maths #4

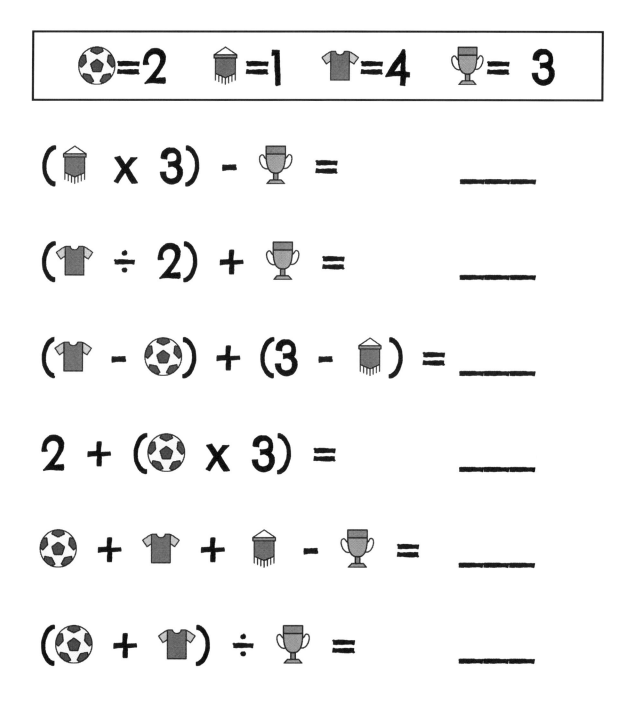

$$\text{⚽} = 2 \quad \text{🚩} = 1 \quad \text{👕} = 4 \quad \text{🏆} = 3$$

(🚩 x 3) - 🏆 = _____

(👕 ÷ 2) + 🏆 = _____

(👕 - ⚽) + (3 - 🚩) = _____

2 + (⚽ x 3) = _____

⚽ + 👕 + 🚩 - 🏆 = _____

(⚽ + 👕) ÷ 🏆 = _____

Answers on page 66

Design a Keeper's Gloves

The keeper in your team wants some new gloves. Can you colour in the ones below so that they look amazing?

Which Route to the Stadium?

Can you draw a route to help the fans reach the ground? Remember to follow the arrows.

FAN BUS

Answer on page 88

ANSWERS

Football Maths #1

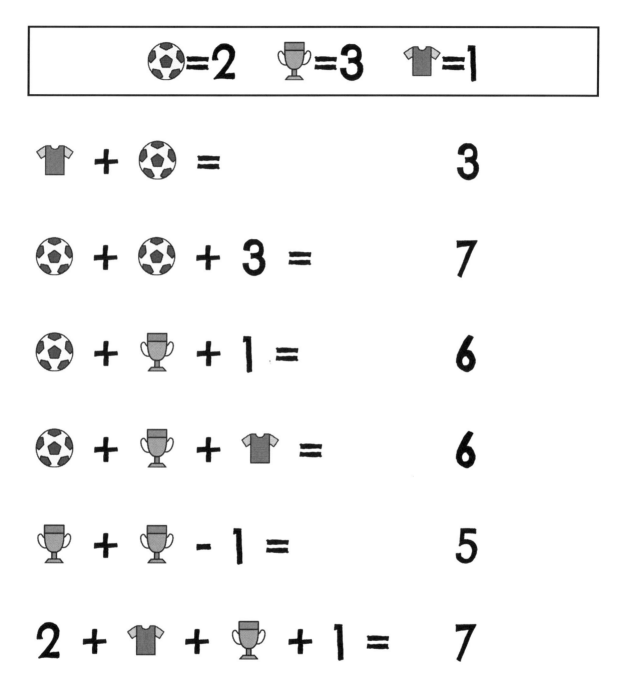

⚽ = 2   🏆 = 3   👕 = 1

👕 + ⚽ =   3

⚽ + ⚽ + 3 =   7

⚽ + 🏆 + 1 =   6

⚽ + 🏆 + 👕 =   6

🏆 + 🏆 - 1 =   5

2 + 👕 + 🏆 + 1 = 7

Football Maths #2

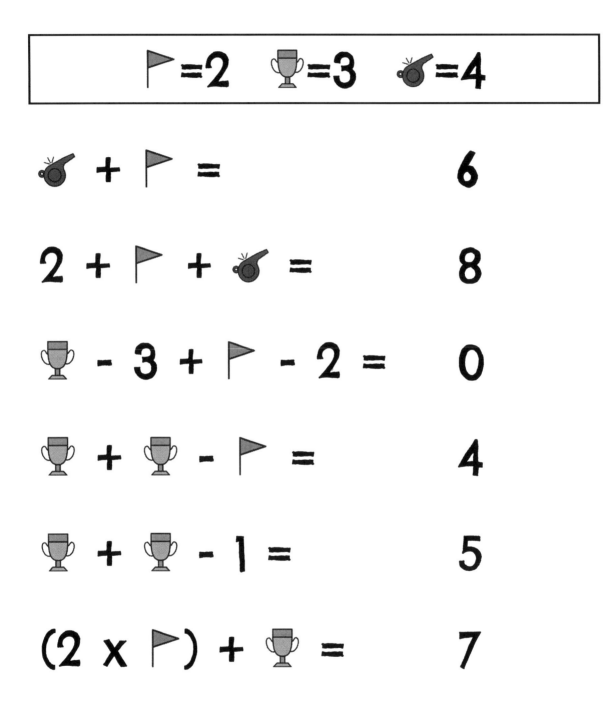

Football Maths #3

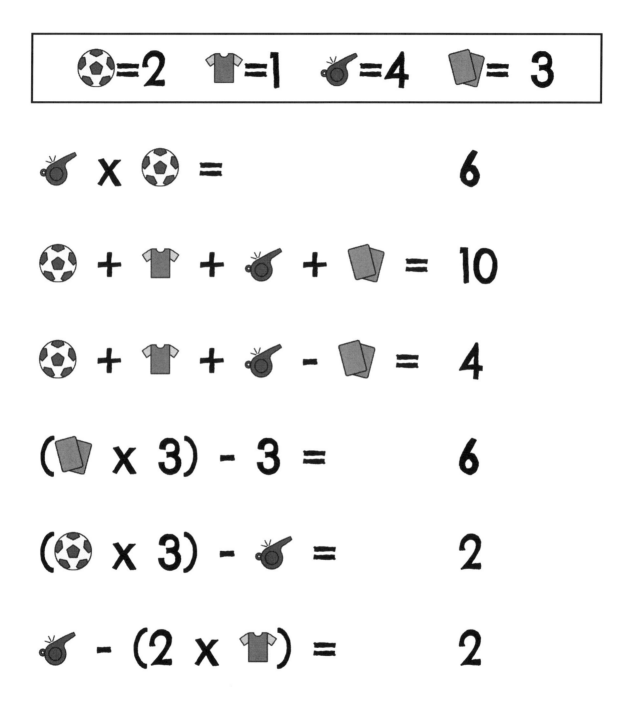

⚽ = 2   👕 = 1   📣 = 4   🃏 = 3

📣 x ⚽ =   6

⚽ + 👕 + 📣 + 🃏 = 10

⚽ + 👕 + 📣 - 🃏 = 4

(🃏 x 3) - 3 =   6

(⚽ x 3) - 📣 =   2

📣 - (2 x 👕) =   2

Football Maths #4

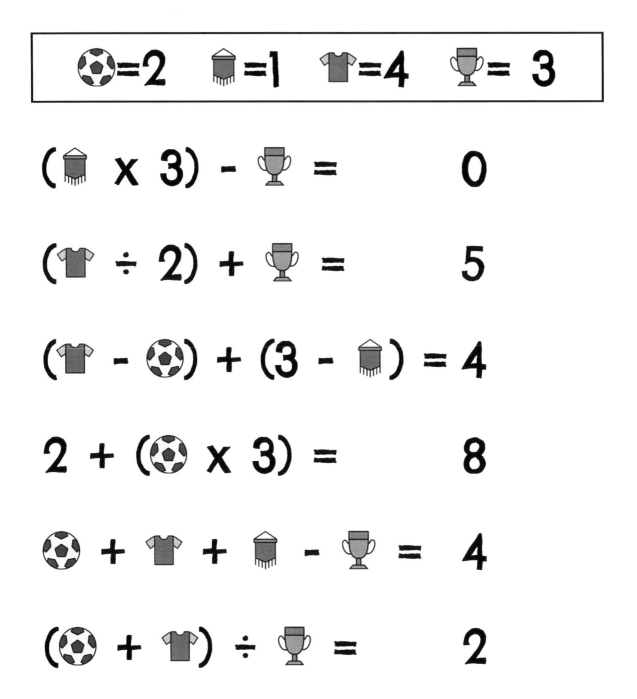

Where on the Map?
Football Stadiums

Liverpool's stadium is number 3

Norwich City's stadium is number 6

Arsenal's stadium is number 8

Cardiff City's stadium is number 7

Aston Villa's stadium is number 5

Southampton's stadium is number 9

Leicester City's stadium is number 4

Celtic's stadium is number 1

Newcastle United's stadium is number 2

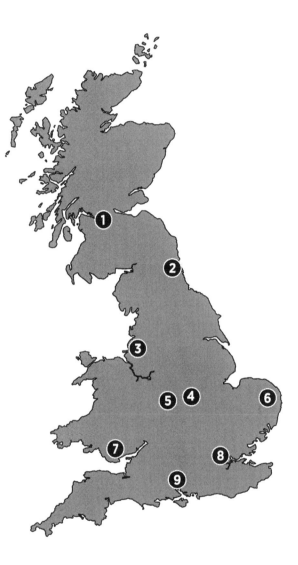

Where on the Map?
European Teams

Spain is country
number 9

Wales is country
number 5

Sweden is country
number 6

Portugal is country
number 11

Scotland is country
number 1

Italy is country
number 10

Northern Ireland is
country number 2

France is country
number 8

England is country
number 4

Germany is country
number 7

Republic of Ireland
is country number 3

Match the Silhouettes

Name That Team #1

Team 1 is Everton.

Team 2 is Norwich City.

Which Line? Can You Score?

Ellie should choose line B.

Spot the Difference

How Many Balls?

Spot the Cliché

The real clichés are in bold. The fakes are crossed out.

Sick as a parrot?	Or	~~Sick as a goat?~~
He plays box to box	Or	~~He plays corner to corner?~~
~~A game of half and half~~	Or	**A game of two halves?**
Early doors	Or	~~Late doors?~~
~~Parking the car~~	Or	**Parking the bus?**
~~Hit the crossword~~	Or	**Hit the woodwork?**
Kick it in Row Z	Or	~~Kick it in Row A?~~
~~Running down the game~~	Or	**Running down the clock?**
~~A windy Wednesday in Wales~~	Or	**A wet Tuesday night in Stoke?**

The Tricky Maze Cup

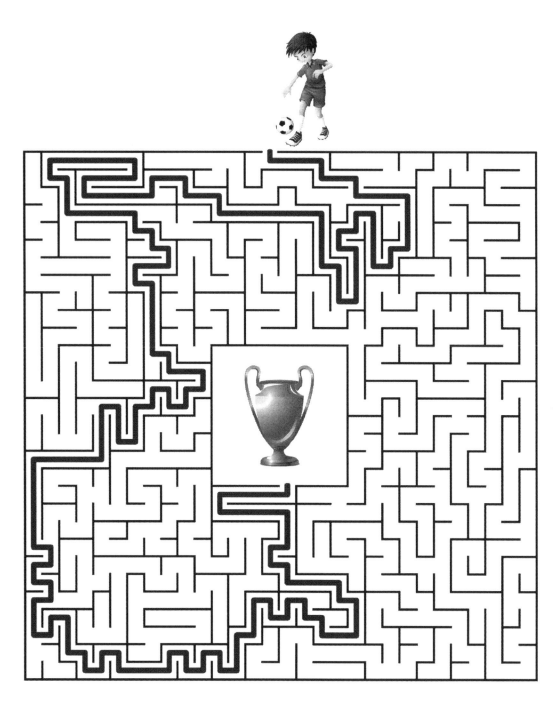

Find the Player

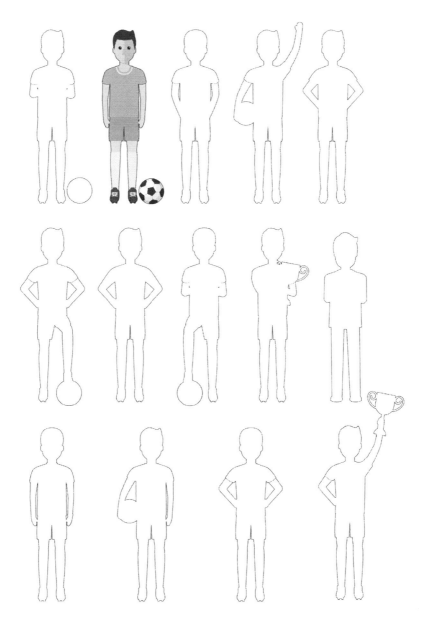

Beat the Defenders!

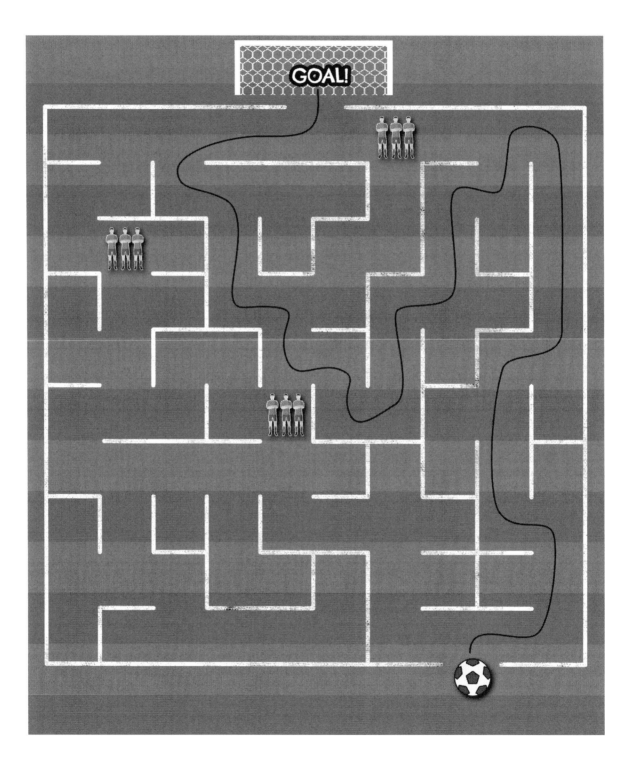

Mixed Up Keepers

1. A Peak Grail Bazaar — Kepa Arrizabalaga

2. Unsung Nag — Angus Gunn

3. A Diva Edged — David de Gea

4. Sore Ned — Ederson

5. Hurl Igloos — Hugo Lloris

6. A Cop Drink Fjord — Jordan Pickford

7. Hip Mackerel Chess — Kasper Schmeichel

8. In Lasso — Alisson

Name That Team #2

Team 3 is Bury.

Team 4 is Southampton.

Which Stadium?

1. Southampton — St Mary's Stadium

2. Liverpool — Anfield

3. Leeds United — Elland Road

4. Leicester City — King Power Stadium

5. Fulham — Craven Cottage

6. Manchester United — Old Trafford

7. Arsenal — Emirates Stadium

8. Burnley — Turf Moor

9. Bournemouth — Dean Court

Secret Code Teams

A	B	C	D	E	F	G	H	I	J	K	L	M	N	O	P	Q	R	S	T	U	V	W	X	Y	Z
M	T	C	E	F	S	O	L	I	D	P	B	A	W	U	V	N	R	Y	Z	G	X	H	Q	K	J

E O H W M A

F U L H A M

M R F D Q M H

A R S E N A L

Q D N C M F B H D   O Q I B D J

N E W C A S T L E   U N I T E D

N D F B   W M A   O Q I B D J

W E S T   H A M   U N I T E D

Q G B B I Q U W M A   E G R D F B

N O T T I N G H A M   F O R E S T

England's Missing Letters

1. Harry Maguire

2. Dele Alli

3. Raheem Sterling

4. John Stones

5. Harry Kane

6. Ross Barkley

7. Marcus Rashford

8. Jadon Sancho

The Internationals

1. Antoine Griezmann — France

2. Luis Suárez — Uruguay

3. Eden Hazard — Belgium

4. James Rodríguez — Colombia

5. David De Gea — Spain

6. Mo Salah — Egypt

7. Riyad Mahrez — Algeria

8. Zlatan Ibrahimovic — Sweden

9. Pierre-Emerick Aubameyang — Gabon

Secret Code Honours

A	B	C	D	E	F	G	H	I	J	K	L	M	N	O	P	Q	R	S	T	U	V	W	X	Y	Z
D	E	Y	W	F	H	A	Z	K	V	S	M	N	I	L	G	X	J	O	T	U	Q	P	R	B	C

EG   ZUW

FA   CUP

BUXSWG   OBGPUB

EUROPA   LEAGUE

WXBLNBX   OBGPUB

PREMIER   LEAGUE

DSXOA   ZUW

WORLD   CUP

ZFGLWNSMK   OBGPUB

CHAMPIONS   LEAGUE

Mixed Up Teams

1. User In Detachment   **Tottenham Hotspur**

2. Scratchy Tie Men   **Manchester City**

3. Love or Lip   **Liverpool**

4. Dun Snarled   **Sunderland**

5. A Lint Salvo   **Aston Villa**

6. Eel Cash   **Chelsea**

7. Never To   **Everton**

8. Ye Kit Cost   **Stoke City**

Match the Pairs

Teams with Missing Letters

1. West Ham United

2. Leicester City

3. Manchester City

4. Liverpool

5. Everton

6. Wolverhampton Wanderers

7. Crystal Palace

8. Manchester United

Name That Team #3

Team 5 is Manchester City.

Team 6 is Leeds United.

Chase for the Ball!

Top Players Word Search #1

```
.   .   .   .   M   .   .   .   .   .   C   .   .   C   .   .
.   .   .   .   .   A   .   .   .   I   .   .   R   .   D
.   .   .   .   .   R   A   .   R   .   .   .   G   I   .   R
.   .   .   .   .   L   C   D   .   .   .   N   .   S   T   A
K   .   L   .   .   I   .   O   E   .   .   O   .   .   T   G   Z
.   Y   .   I   S   .   M   .   .   L   J   .   .   .   I   I   A
S   .   L   S   O   A   .   .   .   E   O   .   .   .   A   L   H
E   .   O   I   K   N   .   .   D   .   .   .   .   N   E   N
R   N   .   U   A   .   E   E   .   .   .   .   .   O   D   E
G   .   L   .   .   N   I   L   .   .   .   .   .   R   S   D
I   .   .   .   .   K   M   .   M   .   .   .   .   O   J   E
O   .   .   .   N   .   .   B   .   E   .   .   .   N   I   .
R   .   .   E   .   .   .   .   A   .   S   .   .   A   H   .
A   .   R   .   .   .   .   .   P   .   S   .   .   L   T
M   F   .   .   .   .   .   .   .   P   .   I   .   D   T   .
O   .   .   .   .   .   .   .   .   E   .   .   O   A   .
S   .   V   I   R   G   I   L   V   A   N   D   I   J   K   M   .
```

Alisson, Matthijs de Ligt, Marcelo, Sergio Ramos, Virgil van Dijk, Frenkie de Jong, Eden Hazard, Luka Modric, Cristiano Ronaldo, Kylian Mbappe, Lionel Messi

Secret Code Players

↵	⇋	⇷	⇄	⇈	⇶	⇲	⇇	⇉	⇈	⇊	∩	↷	↻	↺	↻	↺	↶	⋋	⌃	⌁	⌣	⌣	⇪	⇧	⇦
U	V	T	P	S	H	Y	N	Q	B	W	X	R	F	D	M	J	O	I	K	G	E	Z	A	C	L

⇈ ⌣ ⇇ ↻ ⇧ ↻ ⋋ ⇇　　↻ ⌣ ⇇ ↺ ⇲

B E N J A M I N　　M E N D Y

⇧ ⇧ ⇦ ⇦ ↵ ↻　　⇈ ⋋ ⇦ ⇈ ↺ ⇇

C A L L U M　　W I L S O N

⇧ ⇦ ⌣ ∩　　⋋ ⇈ ↺ ⇈ ⋋

A L E X　　I W O B I

⇈ ⌣ ⇇　　⇧ ⇷ ⋋ ⇦ ⇈ ⌣ ⇦ ⇦

B E N　　C H I L W E L L

↻ ↺ ⇈ ⇈　　⇈ ⇧ ↻ ⌃ ⇦ ⌣ ⇲

R O S S　　B A R K L E Y

Top Players Word Search #2

```
·  D  R  A  N  E  R  E  I  D  N  E  W  ·  ·  ·
·  ·  ·  M  ·  ·  ·  ·  ·  ·  ·  ·  ·  ·  ·  ·
E  ·  ·  A  L  U  C  Y  B  R  O  N  Z  E  ·  ·  ·
L  ·  ·  N  ·  M  E  G  A  N  R  A  P  I  N  O  E
L  ·  ·  D  ·  ·  ·  ·  ·  ·  Z  ·  ·  ·
E  ·  ·  I  ·  ·  ·  ·  ·  ·  T  ·  ·  ·
V  ·  ·  N  ·  ·  ·  ·  A  ·  R  ·  ·  ·
A  ·  ·  E  ·  ·  ·  L  ·  ·  E  ·  ·  ·
L  ·  ·  H  ·  ·  ·  E  ·  ·  E  ·  ·  ·
E  ·  ·  E  M  ·  X  ·  ·  ·  I  ·  ·  ·
S  ·  ·  N  A  M  ·  ·  ·  ·  L  ·  ·  ·
O  ·  ·  R  O  R  ·  ·  ·  ·  U  ·  ·  ·
R  ·  ·  Y  R  ·  T  ·  ·  ·  J  ·  ·  ·  ·
·  ·  ·  G  N  I  L  L  A  F  I  S  C  H  E  R  ·
·  ·  A  ·  ·  ·  ·  ·  ·  ·  ·  ·  ·  ·  ·
·  N  ·  ·  ·  K  E  L  L  E  Y  O  H  A  R  A  ·
S  A  R  I  V  A  N  V  E  E  N  E  N  D  A  A  L
```

Sari van Veenendaal, Lucy Bronze, Nilla Fischer, Kelley O'Hara, Wendie Renard, Julie Ertz, Amandine Henry, Rose Lavelle, Marta, Alex Morgan, Megan Rapinoe

Which Route to the Stadium?

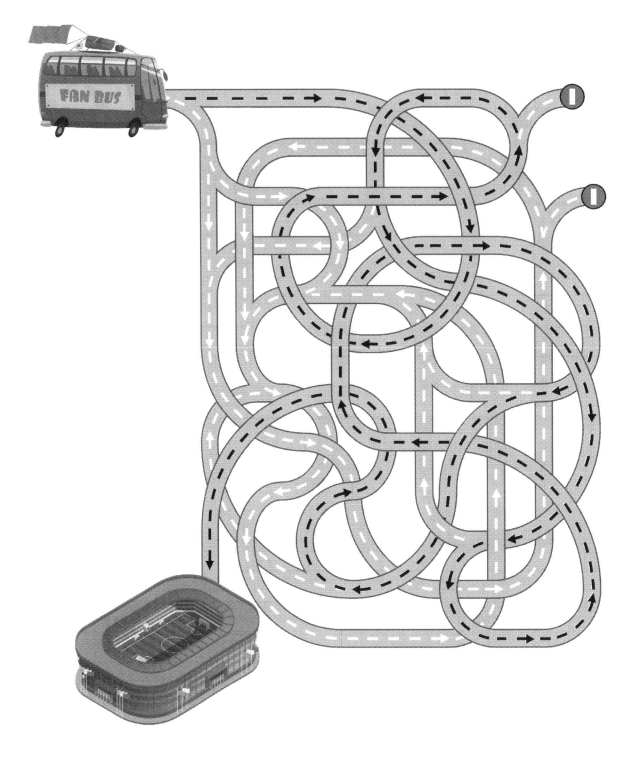

Premier League Word Search

```
·  ·  ·  E  ·  ·  ·  S  E  V  E  N  N  E  B  U  R  ·
·  ·  ·  K  W  I  L  F  R  E  D  N  D  I  D  I  ·  ·
·  ·  ·  A  ·  ·  ·  ·  ·  ·  ·  ·  ·  ·  L  ·  ·  ·
·  ·  ·  N  ·  ·  ·  ·  ·  ·  ·  ·  ·  E  A  ·  ·  ·
·  ·  ·  A  ·  ·  ·  ·  ·  ·  ·  ·  ·  C  I  ·  ·  ·
·  ·  ·  H  ·  ·  ·  ·  ·  ·  ·  ·  ·  I  T  ·  ·  ·
·  ·  ·  T  ·  ·  ·  ·  ·  ·  ·  ·  ·  R  R  ·  ·  ·
·  ·  ·  A  K  A  H  X  T  I  N  A  R  G  N  A  L  ·
·  ·  ·  N  ·  ·  ·  ·  ·  ·  ·  ·  A  M  U  ·  ·
·  ·  ·  ·  ·  ·  ·  ·  ·  ·  ·  ·  L  Y  C  ·  ·
·  ·  ·  ·  ·  ·  ·  ·  ·  ·  ·  ·  C  N  A  ·  ·
·  Z  E  M  O  G  E  O  J  ·  ·  ·  E  O  S  ·  ·
·  ·  ·  ·  ·  ·  ·  ·  ·  ·  ·  ·  D  H  M  ·  ·
·  B  E  R  N  A  R  D  O  S  I  L  V  A  T  O  ·
·  ·  ·  ·  ·  ·  ·  ·  ·  ·  ·  ·  N  U  ·  ·
·  ·  ·  ·  ·  ·  ·  ·  ·  ·  ·  ·  A  R  ·  ·
·  ·  ·  ·  M  A  H  A  R  B  A  Y  M  M  A  T
```

Nathan Aké, Bernardo Silva, Rúben Neves, Anthony Martial, Lucas Moura, Tammy Abraham, Granit Xhaka, Joe Gomez, Wilfred Ndidi, Declan Rice

Top Teams Word Search #1

```
D E T I N U R E T S E H C N A M ·
N · H Y · · · · · · · · · · S ·
O · G T · · · · · · · · · H ·
R · U N · · · · · · · · · E Y
W · O U · A · · · · · · · F T
I · R O N · R · · · · · · F I
C · B C · O · S · · · · · I C
H · S Y · · T · E · · · · E R
C · E B · · · P · N · · · L E
I · L R · · · · M · A · · D T
T · D E · · · · · A · L · U S
Y · D D · · · · · · H · · N E
· · I · · · · · · · · T · I C
· · M · · · · · · · · U · T I
· · · · · · · · · · · O · E E
D E T I N U M A H T S E W · S D L
D E T I N U S D E E L · · · · · ·
```

Manchester United, Arsenal, West Ham United, Leeds United, Middlesbrough, Derby County, Sheffield United, Southampton, Leicester City, Norwich City

Stadiums Word Search

```
S T A M F O R D B R I D G E · · K
· · T H E H A W T H O R N S K · I
· · · · · · · · · · · R · · R
· · · · · · · · · K A · · · K
· · · · · · · · R P · · · K L
· · · · · · · A N D · · · R E
· · · · · · P O A · · · A E
· · · · · S S O D · · · P S
· · · · E I R A · · K · T S
· · · · M D E O · · R · S T
· · · A O G R · · A · · R A
· · · J O A W · · P · · · U D
· · T G R O · · A · · · H I
· S · A R · · L · · · · L U
· C R · · L · · · · · · E M
· I A M O L I N E U X · · · S ·
V C · · V · · · · · · · · · · ·
```

St James' Park, Vicarage Road, Villa Park, Stamford Bridge, Kirklees Stadium, Goodison Park, Molineux, Carrow Road, Selhurst Park, The Hawthorns

European Teams Word Search

```
. . A . . . . . . S . . . . .
. . T . . . . . U . . . . . .
. . L . . . . T . . . . . . .
B . E . . . N . . . . . . . .
A . T . . . E . . . . D . . H
R . I . . V . . . . I . . . C
C . C . U . . I . R . . . . I
E . O J . . L . O D . . . . N
L . M . . O . A T . . . . . U
O . A . P . M . R . . . . . M
N . D . A . L . . O . . . . N
A . R N . A . . . . P . . . R
. . I . E . . . . . . . . . E
. . D . R . . . S E V I L L A Y
D N U M T R O D A I S S U R O B A
. . . . . . . . . . . . . . B
P A R I S S A I N T G E R M A I N
```

Barcelona, Bayern Munich, Juventus, Atlético Madrid, Paris Saint-Germain, Real Madrid, Borussia Dortmund, Napoli, Porto, Sevilla

Thank you!

I hope you enjoyed the book.

If you'd like to message me about anything, my email is

harrykayebooks@gmail.com

Hope your team wins their next game!

Harry

Printed in Poland
by Amazon Fulfillment
Poland Sp. z o.o., Wrocław

61186645R00061